WINNING!

Success in the Construction Industry

Richard A. Reese

WINNING!

Success in the
Construction Industry

Richard A. Reese

Written Words Publishing LLC

Written Words Publishing LLC
P.O. Box 462622
Aurora, Colorado 80046
www.writtenwordspublishing.com

Published by Written Words Publishing LLC April 4, 2026.

ISBN: 978-1-961610-45-3 (paperback)
ISBN: 978-1-961610-47-7 (hardcover)
ISBN: 978-1-961610-46-0 (eBook)

Library of Congress Control Number: 2026938233

Cover designed by Written Words Publishing LLC

Manufactured and printed in the United States of America

TABLE OF CONTENTS

ACKNOWLEDGEMENTS

Listening and learning from others are essential ingredients of success. This book reflects the lessons I have learned over so many years and those with whom I have been associated. Many ideas deemed useful and beneficial for you are interwoven within the fabric of this book's recommendations. Great appreciation is expressed, and respect acknowledged, for those named and unnamed contributors.

I also express heartfelt thanks to my wife, Bette, our daughter, Sheryl, son-in-law, Paul, and daughter, Julie G., for their technical assistance, and to my civil engineer friend, Andy Romance, who provided early input.

FOREWORD

When Richard "Dick" Reese asked me to write a foreword for his book *Winning: Success in the Construction Industry*, I was honored, surprised and apprehensive. We have known each other for a long time and have discovered over countless conversations that we have many common experiences and values.

Nobody can tell a story better than a practitioner. Dick has "been there/done that" in the field of construction. *Winning: Success in the Construction Industry* is a compilation of decades of project experience as an owner, contractor and program manager. Anyone who is in the field has had successes and failures. Dick guides us through techniques to complete any project on time and on budget.

After my initial surprise at being asked, I realized he asked partly because, like him, I am an engineer having graduated from the University of Nevada, Reno with a degree in Civil Engineering. My background includes work in both the public and private sector, as well as being the owner representative on several projects for over 50 years. I have also served four terms as Mayor of a midsized Arizona community, giving me a unique viewpoint on what makes a successful project.

Dick has talked for a long time about writing a book to help all project team members work together to complete projects successfully. This book's primary theme is the need for communication among all involved. Everyone has their own needs within a project. So many failed projects have poor communication resulting in team members having different agendas. The key is to make sure the owner ultimately gets the product they expected, the contractor makes a profit and the architect/engineer is satisfied that the end result/product is safe and represents their design.

Too many projects get off track at some point and the team forgets they are all responsible for completing it on time and on budget. *Winning: Success in the Construction Industry* will provide you with a summary of 50 years of experience that will help in the ultimate goal of a successful project.

This is a quick and easy read with lots of valuable tips. Read, enjoy and practice!

Written by Robert Jackson, Mayor (retired)

INTRODUCTION

Those who fall under any of the following categories will find this tool useful:

- Architects
- Design Engineers
- General Contractors
- Subcontractors
- Public and Private Sector Owners
- Specialty Consultants
- Developers
- Entrepreneurs
- Project Managers
- Program Managers
- Construction Managers
- Lenders
- Venture Capitalists
- Land Use Attorneys
- Elected Officials
- Municipal Department Heads
- Citizen Stakeholders and those who have fulfilled successful careers and now fondly reminiscing with lightheartedness.

I, Richard A. Reese, worked on writing this book for quite some time, handwriting notes about WINNING IN THE CONSTRUCTION BUSINESS, building long-term relationships with repeat clients. Of course, I've continuously reminded myself that a book must be written to benefit others, not myself. I don't want to release a book and, at the end of the day, be the only one who possesses it, having a garage full to satisfy my ego trip.

So, suspecting the any/all thoughts, ideas, postulates have been conceived and probably published before, I've tried to find anything that speaks, with clarity and succinct expression, to the concept of winning. I found there is nothing and, in further support of that conclusion, read something published by someone smarter than I am. I concluded that the construction industry ranks dead last in communication skills.

When you are in the business of real estate development or you are a planner, owner, architect, engineer, subcontractor, general contractor, or supplier, you are an important player in the efforts "to convert dreams into income streams." You start each day intending to serve or earn profit from making a quantifiably important professional contribution to a project's bottom-line success.

Me? I've been where you are, in more than a few of those roles, and at this point in my life want to offer help with insight, direction, inspiration, and encouragement. I aim to provide thoughts you can use to move faster and more profitably toward your goals.

So, how do I do that with this book? How can I best serve you? How can your time be invested, not wasted? Answer: Each page must represent a rung in a success ladder for you. Thoughts shared must be either very important reminders of how to or be new input, directions and strategies for you to use quickly.

So, here we go!

CHAPTER ONE

PREPARATION

It takes planning, attitude, relationships, and commitment to complete a successful project on time and on budget. Let's examine each of these areas.

Planning

We've all heard, "Failing to plan is planning to fail." So:

- ❖ Write your plan down.
- ❖ Be brief, reasonable, strategically creative, and focused.
- ❖ Whether talking about a Business Plan for your company or a plan to win a specific job, think about the basics.

Distill the fundamentals in an outline, no matter what business you're in or the nature of the job you are competing to win. Be sure to address administration, operations, marketing, and finance similar to the following:

<u>Administration</u>: We are a lean, efficient team. We rank lowest in our industry in terms of operating overhead, enhancing our ability to compete and WIN without laying a burden on the client to pay for more than needed to exceed expectations.

<u>Operations</u>: We pledge the team members who are best suited to each job. The experience of our people matches or exceeds the performance demands of the client.

<u>Marketing</u>: Our brochures, data sheets, sales aids, and proposals are succinct—no fluff— truthful portrayals of relevant company and project team qualifications. We pursue client relationships that enable us to excel in our performance. We tailor and focus our marketing efforts—from cold calling to winning repeat client relations—on earning professional respect and the privilege of long-term relationships.

<u>Finance</u>: Our financial strength, measured by full disclosure and bank to bank communications, bonding capacity, and industry organization rankings, is open to client scrutiny. Our mission is exceptional service and performance, and financial stability is key. Paying our bills on time, earning the respect of our suppliers, translate to starting a job on time, completing it

on schedule and earning the privilege of serving again.

Attitude

Attitude toward winning can be critical to short and long-term success in pursuing a given client, a project or building a business! Work with me on this: I'm not suggesting you chase everything, or ignore realisms, or betray your firm's mission statement, or your principal's direction. I'm just reminding you that the right attitude, the winning one, can be a driver. Someone said: "Success comes in cans, not cannots!"

Relationships

Remember when statutes that governed how publicly funded projects must be awarded "to the lowest responsible bidder?" And, to the General Contractor, that meant licensed and bondable; not a prohibitable hill to climb. Well, while statute authors may have been well meaning, meeting those criteria was so often not a challenge, so the Owner would contract with the lowest monetary bidder, perhaps including 'Joe Jackleg' who left something out of his bid, ready to lay a change order on the Owner before the ink was even dry on his contract!

So now, after generations of disputes, litigation, and mediation, statutes were changed to allow for professional qualifications to govern, i.e., relevant project experience, references, financial strength, and individual experience, leading to elimination of cost overruns, adversarial disputes, etc. What soon followed were contracting method shifts, bringing the General around the table, so to speak, for a fee, to help control costs and time during design, helping the architect to distill out change order risks, 'drawing the lines' once, etc., i.e., 'negotiated' form of contract, now called Construction Manager at Risk (CMAR). So, you, the reader, recognize that the Owner wants to trust his project team members as fiduciaries, acknowledging value of sincere efforts to apply respective skills to each individual team member and Owner benefit.

Commitment

I read an article recently, written by a successful businessman I admire, in which he quoted the old saying, "It's not what you know that counts, it's who you know." I say NOT QUITE; it's not who you know that counts, it's who you GET to know that counts.

We've all known name droppers. Question: how many times has that person whose name you dropped called you? In your gut, in your quiet time, as you cite and rank the names of the prospective clients most important to you, how well do you really know them? Certainly, you can identify the prospects most in common with your core competencies as professionals. You are able to name the top 12 prospective clients in the market you are best able to serve. So, what's left?

How about using the Pareto Principle: 'Concentrate on the vital few and eliminate the trivial many.' Or how about applying the 80/20 rule: 80% of the business—regardless of the business you're in—is commonly done by 20% of the people. So, focus on the 20%, always consistent with honest definition of professional abilities to serve them, performing better than anyone else.

Okay, now that we agree on making a commitment to plan, focus and the importance of relationships, prioritizing them, and investing in building them via hunting with a rifle vs. flock shooting, what's left to be stressed? Let's examine empathy, exceptionalism and target markets.

Empathy

At every level of prospective client interface, your people must put themselves in the viewers', the listeners' heads. Not being stupid, obnoxious or unethical; simply planning marketing efforts around how you would want to be sold, if the situation were reversed.

Exceptionalism

Really, who are you? What are the 'Points of Difference': you, your local office, your company, compared to your competition? Look in the mirror, define and rank the strengths you represent in the world of your clients.

Target Markets

"Go where the business is, not where it ain't," someone said. You have limited time and money to invest in building your business; it is hugely important that you DEFINE your target markets, right to the individual prospects, and marry that definition with an objective analysis of your core competencies. Then focus, not flock shoot, on that 20%.

Business Building Strategies

Now, let's think outside the box. Are there different strategies to build a business that do not require inordinate or extra cost? The answer is yes. It can be accomplished by taking the following actions:

❖ Join or form a 'Tip Club,' a group of non-competing people who meet, say weekly or twice a month, to share 'what's new' and how to help one another. Trust me, such an activity led to much new business. Key is identifying people who are in senior positions or are on their way to more influential responsibilities in the business community. Ideal participants are bankers, attorneys, financial advisors, and others in the construction industry with whom you do not compete, etc.

❖ Build relationships with 'economic development' staff members who work for cities, towns, states, and even federal government, people responsible for bringing new business to their communities. This extends to elected officials who serve in the areas of growth which you have identified in your business plan.

❖ Create a project. Rather than relying so much on subscription lead sheets, the 'Dodge Report,' etc., collaborate with other, non-competing and complimentary professionals to consider ways/means for answering capital improvement needs in areas of growth. Best, current example I can think of may be "P3" (Public Private Partnership)—forming a select team of architects, engineers, a professional public sector financial advisor, and a developer to propose a private sector response to a capital program need (i.e., transportation, water treatment, health care).

So true is it that commonly public sector staffers do not have funds for capital projects; 'public works' is the department most often burdened with providing facilities and services without adequate funds. City managers wring their hands, trying to convince city councils to appropriate money; public push-back ("we don't need bigger government;" "we can get along," etc., etc.) presents another roadblock. Formerly called 'Privatization,' starting in the 90's, the term Public Private Partnership or 'P3' was adopted, wherein the private sector team member brings their money to the need in partnership with government. The U.S. is way behind the UK and Canada, but we're catching up. Infrastructure needs are everywhere and it is the thoughtful architect, general contractor, etc., who learns of a capital need and seeks investors to team, ideally in unsolicited proposals, to form P3's! One more strategy in this regard: contact the Council for Public Private Partnerships in Washington D.C. to learn more!

❖ Consider shifting a portion of the existing internal staff from traditional approaches to providing services as a General Contractor. For example, embark on serving public and private sector prospects as the Program Manager or Owner Representative. Often, the public sector Owner is short-staffed and prohibited by a Board of Supervisors or Council from hiring more people.

While it is true that you would close out the opportunity to be the General Contractor on a given project, consider what may be a way to capture new revenues from a much lower risk contract. (Yours truly did just that by forming a subsidiary company and building a large Program Management business).

Self-Improvement Strategies

Recognizing that teams of any number of people must consist of individuals who are dedicated to growing in the business via constant learning and a commitment to improving their skills, personal and professional. If you need reminders to accept that premise, here are a couple:

❖ A famous football coach said, "Show me a good loser and I'll show you a loser."

❖ "It's not how much it's worth that counts, it's how much someone thinks it's worth." (So, consider your worth to the company, the team, etc., and how you and your contribution need to be perceived.)

Think it! Deliver honest introspective reflections about personal strengths and goals. What a shame that some people spend a lifetime trying to get better at something they'll never be good at. We're not what we think we are—but what we think, we are!

Speak it! Develop communication skills. Steve Jobs and Bill Gates agree that interpersonal communication skills lead to the best chances for success. You can achieve this by contacting the regional headquarters of Toastmasters and/or Dale Carnegie. Find or form a chapter.

Sell it! How sick is it that some professionals, even today in such a competitive world, think that 'selling' is a four-letter word. Nonsense: consider it a fact that if nothing is sold, all the other people (in a company, on a project team, etc.) will have nothing to do! Yes, there are strong arguments in favor of requiring each employee's commitments of personal/ professional probity/integrity, superior skills, loyalty, etc., but still, someone must ask the prospective client: Will you buy this thing? That's Selling 101.

Here are some additional, good, old fundamentals that will never go away:

- The easiest business to get is the business you've already got. Consider vertical and horizontal penetration of existing client relationships by offering additional services. You can also confer with the client about how and with whom you can grow penetration of the market you are currently serving, being careful not to come across as greedy or disrespectful of the current relationship. Author Michael LeBouf wrote, "It costs eight times more to procure a new customer than it does to preserve an old one."

- Expand your network while growing your professionalism. Consider joining professional associations such as APWA (American Public Works Association), PMI (Project Management Institute), ULI (Urban Land Institute), and/or ASHE (American Society of Healthcare Engineers).

- To the A/E professionals: how often do you consider 'Additional Services,' not just to capture a reasonable fee from an existing contract, but in an effort to help your client by being sure to consider scope, systems, material, method, and issues, which do indeed add value to the Owner's program? A specific example from personal experience: Imagine a $500 million, multi-cited capital program planned by a public sector owner having in-house project management staff; imagine the staffers were instructed to get on with hiring architects, design, bid, build, occupy, etc. Now, imagine that the A/E RFP's did not include accurate definition of space ('program') sufficient for long and short-listed firms to submit responsible proposals.

Question: wouldn't this set of circumstances suggest this owner could benefit from outside help? Yes, and I provided that help, proposing, in this instance, to be a Program Management consultant, providing the service of Programming, Budget, Schedule, and staff augmentation. Note: this owner was prohibited from hiring more people, while recognizing professional shortcomings and risk of bad management of a massive capital program. So, going 'outside' was an answer—commissioning a consultant to come on board to help ensure success. The engagement lasted four years; the client awarded us a gold star and sole source consideration for future work.

The Interview

Most governmental organizations hire A/E consulting professionals with a Qualifications Based Selection (QBS) process. Following that lead, now more often, a General Contractor is also selected with similar steps; that is a 'negotiated contract' method is used, currently called Construction Manager at Risk (CMAR), whereby short-listed firms are invited to interviews. Based on interview grading, final selections are made. So, the importance of the interview cannot be overstated.

Following are tips for WINNING:

- Each person who attends the interview should have a speaking part. Yes, the boss, President and Principal should attend and speak, perhaps to introduce the team and confirm importance of the job…BUT NOT RUN OFF AT THE MOUTH. The Owner wants to hear from the people who will perform the work.

- Avoid relying on PowerPoint presentations. Personally, I'm against over-reliance on this tool to sell a job! How about using flip charts in lieu or in addition to? This is a people business to such a great degree; the Owner is about to 'make a marriage' for a lengthy duration. The project may be the most important money commitment the Owner has ever made (or the A/E and General Contractor might be smart to assume that to be the case).

  The speaker should stand to the side of the projected image, making eye contact with the audience, referring to the image detail (usually bullet points) by placing a hand on the screen or wall where the projection of each item is being made, looking briefly at the point being made and then returning to look at the audience and speak. Rehearse this and then rehearse again.

- Get creative; not cute, just different in ways that lend support to an Owner's thinking that 'this is the team I want on my job!' Here's a real-world example: the job was a major addition to a large, existing building. Our Project Manager contacted the Owner well before the interview to obtain as-built drawings. Then, using tissue overlay, we showed how we would accomplish the work of integrating the new construction without risk of interrupting existing operations. We spoke about safety, design compatibility and schedule, demonstrating ability to accomplish the work within the Owner's budget and timelines. The Owner was positively impressed. It was as if we had already started work and we got the job!

CHAPTER TWO

MARKETING

◆

Please try (for some, a very tough challenge all by itself) to keep your mind open—no preconceived opinions or notions, no prejudices, no baggage! MARKETING is not a four-letter word! But believe it or not, there are some teachers and professionals in the business who still expect that putting your name in a directory is enough. They operate on the mindset that "the Owner, the client will find us."

So, you are open to considering marketing to be an honorable, essential component of your overall efforts to build a successful business as an architect or engineer, a general contractor, a subcontractor, a developer, a supplier, a program manager, etc.? Believe me, that mindset of openness will serve you well as we "explode" the word and see how marketing successfully can contribute to your succeeding in business profitably!

First, marketing is the big word. It includes market research, planning, public relations, advertising, and sales.

Market Research

This element of a good marketing plan may be more relevant to the Developer than others who are in the construction game. It involves knowing growth trends in a given geographic area of economic development: commercial, industrial, hospitality, residential, and retail.

Question: is there a market for more? What is the current absorption? What is the political climate for that first project or more? For all others in the game, however, it is still important to know the territory—defining the economic climate so as NOT to waste time and money chasing ghosts but investing wisely in new business pursuits.

Planning

Whatever your specialty, 80% of the business is being done by 20% of the people. Ask yourself the following questions:

- Who are they who enjoy the 80%?
- What do they have that sells?
- What have they done to get there?

- Do I just copy them in my firm's service offerings?

Answer: maybe so; maybe that is the ticket. Or perhaps NOT, since the client has a relationship with that competitor and simply proposing the same services without giving the prospective client reasons to change horses will probably NOT be enough incentive.

Your competitor owns that relationship. It is your obligation to help that prospect decide to entertain change! So 'look in the mirror'; as earlier considered, what are the "Points of Difference"? What distinguishes you? What are the discriminators? What can differentiate us in our efforts to get the prospective client's attention and hold it long enough to win at least that first shot at being a service provider?

Some 'P.O.D.'s to consider:

- We are well prepared.
- We have depth of resources.
- We are more creative, competitive, earnest, and professionally certified.
- We are supported by clients whose testimonials confirm our ability to repeatedly perform well!

Public Relations

Perhaps, especially for the A/E's, Developers, General Contractors, and Program Managers, knowing the best P/R firms can save time and money when making important decisions such as:

- Do we pursue a given client?
- Is this an area of growth?
- How did my competitor get the business I want?
- What are the prospective client's hot buttons?
- What do I do to get attention, hold it and win?
- What organizations should we focus on, join, participate in?

A good P/R firm knows them all and has influence to use in starting at the top. Regarding public sector client prospects, the right P/R firm will put you into relationships they have, which will save cold call dollars, and they will assist with getting your message to the decision makers, etc.

Advertising

Trust me, it's so easy to reject thoughts about spending money to advertise. I understand the reluctance, especially in a young, maybe start-up business when it is critical to spend greatly limited funds wisely! So, do you advertise or not? Answer: yes, under the following circumstances:

- The client uses the publication to identify firms/companies to consider (i.e., ASHE in the health care market, ULI, perhaps the most prestigious economic development organization in the U.S., and APWA, an organization of public works officials).

- There is an event planned by your prospect or an event in which your prospect will take part, perhaps as a sponsor, panelist or community leader. Placing the right ad can help when it's proposal time.

Here's a real-life story to help you reconcile spending money to advertise:

Many years ago, at a national convention of advertisers, held at the Fairmont Hotel in San Francisco, Napoleon Hill, a famous author, was asked to speak on the three most important principles of advertising. He accepted the offer, charging $10,000. He stepped to the lectern and said: "The three most important principles of advertising are: REPETITION, REPETITION, REEITITION." Then he left the stage and sat down. Of course, the convention sponsors were shocked…but the message stuck!

Sales

Wow! So many things come to mind, but you know what? I'd bet you know what they are. You could 'write the book' about do's and don'ts; you know the best salesman from all the rest; you've been there and done that. I don't want to waste your time but I do want to help you define success in sales and selling. So, here are a few important things to think about:

1. The best salesperson in professional services is one who obviously has 'walked the walk,' not just talked the talk. This is the individual who knows the client's interests and needs, can cut to the chase vs. extraneous talk in that cold call (having done homework about the prospect and the project). He/she couldn't respect more the value of relationships and makes it obvious with words, literature and, ultimately, a proposal that the firm/company seeks the privilege of earning trust, faith and respect via performance and the opportunity for there to be a long-term client relationship.

2. Treat the receptionist with respect and courtesy. You have one opportunity to make a good first impression. You never know what that person's relationship may be with

the individual you are trying to reach or meet with, etc.

3. 'Ask for the order'…not being shy, but friendly and serious, confirming your preparedness to hit the ground running in addressing the client's concerns, most pressing issues, etc. (i.e. time, quality, budget, safety).

Following are two, not uncommon scenarios for you to consider from a 'marketing' perspective:

<u>Situation #1</u>: An open, honest, well thought out decision to respond to an RFP leaves you concluding that you do not have the best chance to win. You have thoughts such as: our people get experience in preparing, perhaps making the short list, exposing our strengths to the client such that next time that client will know us. Understand that I am not advocating chasing ghosts, wasting precious time/money, or risking impact on esprit de corps. I'm just asking that you consider the old saying: "Are we better off risking loss realistically than never having tried?"

<u>Situation #2</u>: You won! You got the job! As architects, engineers, PM/Owner Reps, etc., let's assume you currently have one or more contracts for services with your clients. And let's assume you were commissioned to provide specific services, reflected in RFPs to which you responded with winning proposals; you have

commenced work on these contracts and perceive opportunities to add 'additional services' for the benefit of your clients.

So commonly, thoughts about such services pretty much track or are just extensions of the work you already have under way. Well, I suggest there are opportunities for you to add benefits to your clients via what we'll call vertical or horizontal penetrations of the existing service offerings.

*VERTICAL: See the Standard Form of Agreement Between Design-Builder and Architect for a Traditional Design-Build Project published by the AIA (Document B141), suggested for use by architects with their Owner clients re: "The Owner's Program." While, yes, the language that follows allows or implies that the architect may participate in development of the program, but what if there is no "program," or definition of space, according to which the architect can proceed responsibly to perform work on Preliminary Drawings or CD's, detailed plans and specifications?

Section 1.1.2.5 of the agreement states "The financial parameters are...amount of the Owner's budget for the project..."[1] Question: what if there

---

[1] AIA Contract Documents, "B141-2024 Standard Form of Agreement Between Design-Builder and Architect for a Traditional Design-Build Project," accessed March 1, 2026, at: https://aiacontracts.com/documents/b141-2024.

is no budget that you can use, confidently, according to which your work on design can proceed with assurance of confidence that the budget is accurate? Might there be opportunity for you to propose validation so as to assure no errors or omissions?

*HORIZONTAL: Not uncommonly, owner organizations, perhaps especially in connection with larger public sector owners, will include operations and maintenance or alterations and improvement departments dedicated to performing services needed to keep facilities and equipment in optimum operating condition, performing maintenance and repair functions, etc. Such departments can include the full range of service capabilities, from simplest janitorial and building maintenance functions to elevator technicians, 'tin knockers,' HVAC technicians, roofers, glazers, finish carpenters, etc. So, question to you: isn't it fair, isn't it consistent with your desire, presumably, to serve your client more holistically, to the client's ultimate benefit, to consider how these operating and maintenance functions are being performed, offering counsel, supplementary aid in assuring the Owner's facilities will operate without interruption?

Note, dear reader: At this point, regarding marketing, knowing your industry and yourself, let me relate a personal experience as a testimony that marketing success includes investing oneself in career planning, really knowing the firm/company you work for!

A Los Angeles-based A/E firm, specializing in light industrial work, especially cement plant design projects, led by the son of the deceased founder, had interest in growth, broadening client and market focus. I had finished a 'Nigeria experience,' had been a long-term friend of the son, and #2 in command, who approached me to join him in the firm. I did that, targeted a wider range of light industrial markets, identified Hughes Aircraft, pursued work, won a large project, and served the firm as Project Manager on that project to its successful completion. Shockingly and suddenly, however, the son died, leaving control to the next in command whose entire professional interest and resume were cement plant design. As he announced that the firm would focus entirely on the cement plant market, employees left and, in fairly short order, its doors closed. So, a question for you: would it have been wiser for me to consider the career change more carefully, playing 'what if' games privately, assessing prospects for the firm to grow, including consideration of its management succession plan and the narrow focus of the CEO's successor?

Now, wanting to adhere to the focus of this chapter on MARKETING, we are reminded that one of the fundamental elements of most any business plan, together with Administration, Operations and Finance is, indeed, marketing. Further, I suggested the word marketing is the 'big' word, so to speak, within which is the word 'sales.' Unfortunately, as mentioned earlier, it's too often subordinated or denigrated by professionals in the construction industry. "We're good or best at what we do. Our reputation will speak for itself. Prospective clients will find us. We'll put our name in the yellow pages and that is enough. Etcetera, etcetera." Well, it is indeed a competitive world out there and it is the firm that knows how to SELL that will win. 'Nothing happens until something is sold.' Following are some marketing fundamentals for you to use in crafting your marketing plans:

A. <u>Avoid Barriers</u>. Do not allow barriers in your firm, on a project team, in relationships with suppliers, in client relations, etc. Plan to communicate your goals and objectives well, be understood, ask the tough questions about performance expectations, and seek 'buy-in.' Developing and applying the interpersonal skills you have learned is so important. Both Steve Jobs and Bill Gates said that development of interpersonal skills is key to success!

B. <u>Points of Difference</u>. They do indeed invariably exist within a company, a firm, on a team, etc. Define them, build them into your marketing plan, cite the benefits they represent to your clients, quantify those benefits in terms of time, cost, operating efficiencies, attitude, teamwork.

C. <u>Networking</u>. Identify the organizations with which your firm, professionally, has most in common. Consider assigning who (because of job description, personality, time) would be the best to represent you.

So many examples quickly come to mind, i.e. ASHRAE (American Society of Healthcare Architects and Engineers). Investigate the local chapter, meet with the membership representative, budget time and money required to become not just a casual observer but an active and important member

APWA (American Public Works Association) is another one. Check to see if there is a local chapter, how it is organized, and their composition of membership (public officials vs. vendors). In Los Angeles, there used to be, and may still be, a variety of 'Colleges' available to the members within the chapter. Let's say there is a 'Medical College' and the public sector chapter members having responsibility for medical facilities relate to their programs. You are an architect specializing in healthcare; do we need to say more about interest you may have in chapter membership and activity?

Project Management Institute (PMI) also comes to mind. In interest of brevity, I will refer to a real life experience in which yours truly joined a local chapter of PMI, became president for a term, and got to know a member who was V.P of project management for a national company having sizable, but temporary, capital program needs locally. My firm was devoted 100% to providing professional project management services to such owners and, as the fellow members' staffing needs grew, my firm filled those needs, voiding the alternative of the client's having to hire more staff.

D. <u>Toastmasters International</u>. I hereby stress the importance of learning how to communicate well, both written and oral, and propose that you investigate, learn about benefits, trusting that they can be very important to your firm and you personally. Chapters are often located conveniently near home or office. In a non-threatening environment one can learn speaking techniques, grow in confidence, build relationships, enjoy fellowship, and benefit from improvement of skills needed for enhanced career advancement.

So MARKETING, the 'big' word, does indeed involve a great deal more than strict definition and application to a firm, a company, a team. It includes introspective, personal consideration of likes, wants, career desires, and goal setting.

So, dear readers, closing the comments about this important subject, I challenge you to seek and pursue the best, reasonable goals and objectives, including self-examination, avoiding those times when it's not difficult to respond to an idea, a proposal, an opportunity with a YES BUT! And I put an exclamation point on that because of how such a reaction can steer a conversation and consideration of an idea, a new thought, etc., in a negative direction BEFORE THE IDEA HAS EVEN BEEN DEFINED. So, regarding 'looking in the mirror' and self-examination in context of planning for growth of a company, for example, or considering pursuit of a job, or considering one's personal behavior profile, can be so important. Are you a glass of water that's 'half full' or 'half empty'? Isn't it fair or reasonable to suggest that keeping an open mind, opening with the positive vs. something negative can be beneficial? I'm NOT suggesting injection of something weird, stupid or distracting is okay. I AM suggesting, in those situations wherein a team, for example, may be strategizing pursuit of a goal of any kind, that one make every REASONABLE effort to think positively.

Remember the old story about the boy who was observed to be sorting through a huge pile of horse manure? A bystander passing by asks what he's doing. The boy answers: With all this horse manure, there just has to be a pony in there somewhere!

Chapter Three

Owner Hires

You know that the public or private sector Owner who has made known plans to expand, to add to a capital program or infrastructure project of any scope, is targeted by firms wanting to provide design, construction, legal, project, and program management services. Architects, engineers, and general contractors work so very hard to get that Owner's attention with cold calls, sales materials, networking strategies…each wanting to be first and chosen by the Owner, each driven to WIN! Given that it is the Owner's sole responsibility to select the best service providers, however, might it be true that worse than that Owner's having to sift through the choices would be having no choice at all of whom to hire? Therefore, I urge you to use this book, each chapter, in ways as valued professionals, honoring your purpose to serve through WINNING!

A competitor Architect posted on LinkedIn that an 8-person firm should not advertise diverse architectural "expertise," further asserting that small firms should specialize in only one area of service. The only proposition in support of that argument was the number of employees. Such thinking that quality deliverables are a function of type, size or location of a company is worthy of deeper consideration. The Owner should be disciplined in withholding judgement, going beyond quick or more superficial consideration of competing resources' input. Perhaps using RFP's, the Owner's judgement in making professional competency evaluations should be guided by expanded inquiry and perspective, digging deeper, checking references, obtaining answers to the most relevant questions, i.e. how many years of experience are represented by long and short listed firms' personnel, and for what prior clients have key personnel to be assigned on this project been engaged? So, size of a firm need not guide, or certainly drive the Owner's thinking. The following thoughts support that suggestion.

First, let's consider how the Owner typically thinks when it comes to 'mega' or 'micro.' Or maybe smarter would be considering what competing firms put forth in their proposals and interviews in attempts to persuade the Owner, sell themselves and win a job:

<u>Mega</u>:

1. You have depth of staff; you cannot fail to put forth qualified professionals because of that depth of staff in all disciplines. Not just because of staff depth, right here in the area of your project, you also have the ability to move people from your various offices to fill needs that may occur unexpectedly, assuring zero interruption of work in progress.

2. Your document control and computer-aided design capabilities are state-of-the-art; you have invested over a long time the money it takes to assure rapid response, schedule and budget control, elimination of change orders, and errors and omissions challenges.

    Caution: For the larger, one-stop-shop firms, several of which are not around anymore or are facing challenges in a climate of economic volatility of overhead control and forced reorganization, the burden of planning is a huge consideration. From a marketing perspective, it may be persuasive and sound advantageous to the prospective client that you have the various engineering disciplines in-house. "We have control of staffing that the smaller firms lack, such that we walk down the hall internally to engage the professionals needed for specific assignments; we do not have to go outside, running risks of not having staff to commit to a job when needed." The caution is that maintaining such an organization continuously can cost serious money. What if there isn't work to keep all the disciplines busy, motivated and professionally sharp?

<u>Micro</u>:

1. You are lean on purpose, referring your very competitive fee structures to your clients via the cost advantages of operating efficiencies. You do not need to carry unproductive staff in the various disciplines.

2. You are hungry for opportunities to earn long-term relationships. You cannot afford to fail. You can't 'sweep under the rug' failure of any kind in proving yourself to be not just competitive but best in class.

3. You know and have experience with the four basic contracting methods: Design/Bid/Build; Design/Build; Owner Builder; Construction Manager at Risk (CMAR); experience that is available to you, your client, to consider which method of contracting is indeed best for your project.

4 You have exceptional relationships with general contractors and can anticipate very competitive performance, elimination of risks of change orders, disputes, litigation.

<u>Situation</u>: You are an architect, desiring to compete for a private sector project. You have

spent time and money on deciding to 'go for it.' Why?

- The location of the job is in your firm's backyard!
- The type of job (commercial, industrial, hospitality, etc.) is reasonably consistent with your firm's past project experience.
- You have client references in the same project type.
- You have staff available, with relevant experience, to assign. Prepare a bar chart showing current workload to illustrate your readiness to make this job a priority.
- One or more of your people have relationships with the Owner: Chamber of Commerce, clubs, committees, etc.
- You do NOT have precisely relevant project experience, BUT you have met and overcome obstacles, challenges on past projects, which make this one a 'slam dunk.'
- You have scored high with the city, county, etc., therefore, you've earned Design Review Board familiarity. Design excellence is superior; a qualification of the team being assigned to this job.

Think like an Owner:

A. Obligation to 'turn over the rocks' beyond any feelings or preconceived notions about the firm to select.

B. Involve the 'right' people to consider the long and short-listed architects—users of the space, past project team members whose qualifications were appropriate, resulting in good work.

C. Win or lose, consider what you have to gain in asking the client to meet with you, sharing how the scoring of the interviews went, what were the 'hot buttons,' etc.

Trust me, much can be learned. Let me share a real experience: picture a public sector client; as a General, we did not get the contract award. Thankfully, however, the client was very open and respected our interest in learning more about how the selection went, what considerations were paramount in the Owner's view, etc. Here's what we learned:

❖ References were most important, especially those projects on which the project manager for this job was assigned.

❖ Current workload was this Owner's concern; the competitor showed a chart of existing contracts and how this job fits as a priority.

❖ The competitor who won planned and conducted a 'Vendor Fair,' renting a meeting room in a local hotel, inviting suppliers and city officials to meet with the key personnel, giving staff members opportunity with flip charts to 'show and tell' concerning the firm's history and experience that compares to the current project.

Your author has always been an outspoken advocate of role playing, perhaps especially in training sessions, or preparing for an interview after having been short-listed, etc. So, how about this: your firm—a G.C. or A/E—has made the cut, been notified of schedule for follow-up interview, and is preparing for that interview. In addition to thoughts about who will participate, who will say what, power point, etc., how about role playing? Typically, the owner will welcome you and say the meeting is yours, perhaps after asking if there are any questions. Some of the best interviews then are led by the Project Architect or, in the case of the G.C., the Project Manager. That person states who's who on the team, what function/responsibility each will have and then introduces the principal of the firm whose job is to briefly confirm the importance of the opportunity to serve the client and pledge unconditional success of the total team effort, then turn the interview back to the Project Architect or Project Manager.

At that point, how about that person saying something along the lines of: "Our preparations for this interview included thoughts about how you, the Owner, our client, have gotten this far with your project, plus what are your biggest concerns and priorities…your planning to evaluate what each of the short listed firms brings to the table, expecting to rank the firms based on these interviews. Using the information you provided to us in your RFP, plus knowledge we then gained about you (the company, the city, the county, etc.) we concluded the following:" (Instead of power point, which I'd bet most of your competitors will use, how about flip chart? The PA or PM speaks to items either prepared ahead of time on the chart, or speaks and writes simultaneously: And here, obviously, are assumptions about Owner concerns, etc.)

❖ <u>OWNER</u>: You've labored with expansion of your facilities, this new development and how to finance it, this major remodel, etc., for a long time. Now, you must get on with it!

❖ <u>G.C.</u>: How about the PM's asking the person responsible for scheduling to speak to this issue? And in doing so, how about saying, "To save time, which is money, we propose to consider with you fast-tracking the project, literally working so closely with the architect that we can begin site work before completing working drawings, etc." (Then put a project schedule before the Owner to show how many weeks, months, etc., will be saved. Earlier occupancy leads to earlier revenue generation, etc.) Or, for the A/E or the G.C., "We understand the importance to you of saving time, so we will gladly cooperate, on this steel frame structure, pre-ordering the structural steel on a tonnage basis vs. waiting for final structural design."

Regardless of the size and ranking of a corporation, a single person can make a positive impression. This author has presented at national conferences and proudly represented their employers. However, seen by others are personal characteristics and skills that shine, whether affiliated with a large or small organization. Here is an excerpt from such feedback following a presentation at a national conference:

"Mr. Reese, we've tabulated results from our recent Marketing Conference, and your post-presentation evaluation scores were absolutely superb. We've been in the seminar business since 1975 and observed many a speaker, both inside and outside our organization, and no one has ever received a higher evaluation. This result is more significant than others because most of the attendees were marketing people. This is truly a peer evaluation. And of even more importance is the fact that you are a gentleman. That's a parlay! Many, many thanks."

~ *The Associated General Contractors of America*

To my readers, as I close this chapter for you, how about my emphasizing some more personal character traits that can, indeed, help an Owner to pre-qualify and/or finally select the team members:

- ❖ <u>Humility</u>: Not thinking less of yourself but thinking of yourself less.
- ❖ <u>Empathy</u>: Placing oneself in the other person's position, considering the viewer's or listener's concerns first; using the 'you' word more than 'I.'
- ❖ <u>Integrity/Probity</u>: Never compromising your commitment to tell the truth.

Chapter Four

Programs and Projects

First, let's agree on the true explanation of a MANAGER:

- ❖ A human, not a robot or a published guideline or plan. A 'manager' is indeed a person.
- ❖ A person who is responsible, accountable for defining an organization's goals and communicating those goals to others.
- ❖ A person who builds an organization of appropriate size, recruiting, enlisting, guiding, inspiring employees to be 'all they can be.'
- ❖ A person who is responsible for evaluating results.

And so that you can apply what I will share, let's agree that the 'IT' could be the largest program or project; be a large company, the smallest team that is competing to win a contract, a department, etc. The principles, the characteristics of winning leadership, and the personal and professional qualities of the most successful managers are what winning is all about! And to elaborate as takeaways for you:

- ❖ People need to know they are valued as part of something that has purpose and their defined individual contributions are respected.
- ❖ The best managers recognize they must earn respect through demonstrations of good leadership, communicating clearly, completely, putting oneself in the place of each employee.

At this point, dear readers, let's use examples from the real world of some management trends in considering how many managers it may take to accomplish an organization's goals.

Earlier was a discussion of 'seller doer': obligating each professional in the organization to bring in new clients and perform the work of the contract. In other words: Get out there and sell the job! If you are the company's CFO or head of operations, that sounds good. 'Utilization' is what turns your crank! Keeping the focus on billable hours, commensurate revenues and profitability seems positive. But what if the staffer, a project engineer, a project manager, does not know how to sell? Worse perhaps, what if he or she will not make a cold call or resist learning how to support the firm's marketing folks, guidelines, strategies for converting 'dreams to income streams'? Wise bosses recognize such impediments to growth; they confront them early and do the surgery needed to build stronger teams internally. How do they do that? The following may be useful strategies for growing your organization.

Companies, firms, that enjoy generations of profitable growth can be structured such that growth is a function of bottom-up strategies, meaning the owner and top management, operate as 'servant' leaders from the bottom of an upside-down pyramid, as earlier defined in this book. Robert K. Greenleaf was a corporate executive who became disenchanted with top-down authoritarian leadership styles in major corporations. Leaving the corporate world, he founded Greenleaf Center for Servant Leadership, spending his career consulting to corporate clients, spreading the idea that the best leaders are those who grow the most enduring organizations, profitably, from the bottom up as servant leaders. The servant leader movement continues to grow worldwide.

One more analogy for you to consider in context of how to bring out the best in each and every team member: think about the orchestra conductor and the best concert performance you have ever witnessed. Question: could the conductor play the French Horn, the Tuba, the Piccolo? Answer: perhaps, but not so well as the people who devote so many hours to being the very best that they can be! So, if individual professionals are superior in what they do, why is a conductor needed? If all the musicians know their parts, if all are dedicated to working together, if each has been recruited to participate because of exceptional talent and experience and each is among the top performers in the world, WHY a conductor? Answer: someone must lead, someone must direct the team, someone must help the 'team members,' to be all they can be, together.

Note, at the expense of being a bit redundant, there may remain something that merits emphasis in the area of 'seller doer' and what I'll do is refer to an actual experience or two. What I ask of you is your thinking, very honestly, about if you fit into either of these scenarios. In each situation, by the way, this author was engaged as a consultant, charged to advise about growing the business.

A large, multi-disciplined regional office of a large A/E firm, operating internationally, decided to adopt the seller doer model. Catching me by surprise, since the decision was made quickly and unilaterally, that plan was announced. Nothing was said about interest, concerns, qualifications of staff, etc. Obviously, it was assumed by the head of operations who made the announcement that each individual would be qualified to proceed and cooperate. Well, that was a bad assumption, evidenced by a senior mechanical engineer, a man with much design experience and tenure, not being comfortable with his expanded 'seller doer' responsibilities. You can imagine that it was awkward for me when he approached me to express his concern, saying that he had no experience in selling. I told him I would think about how I can help and get back to him.

At that point, I went to the head of operations and told him, without identifying the individual who confided in me, to say that 'we' may have jumped too quickly and need to make sure all staff will be okay with the new operating protocol. Well, to my disappointment, the response was that "staff will just have to accept and get out there and sell, etc., end of discussion." At that point, I met with the engineer, told him I'd be glad to coach about some business development tasks tied to seller doer, etc. A week later, that good man resigned. Shortly after that, I left the company, disappointed that the regional office V.P. lacked the *^#*^** to get in the act. And, as a p.s. for you, within a month, a senior executive came to the regional office from the U.S. headquarters to fire the division head AND the head of operations.

A second, real life, situation: a regional office head asked if I'd meet with him, his #2 man and a senior V.P. who would be coming to town to consider growing the local operation, how to do that, what to do, who should do what, etc. Of course, I expected that it was of interest to include consideration of my involvement, timing, cost, etc. I'd known the company for many years, respected a long history and appreciated the interest in me. The meeting of the four of us proceeded and you can imagine that the informal agenda began with review of the situation, staffing, goals, competition, bookings/backlog, etc. Throughout, I found it odd that the #2 man, after introductions, said not one word. As we considered the market for the firm's services, something just didn't feel right, so I pitched a curve ball. I asked, "If I were to meet with your employees as a total group and ask, 'How many of you are salesmen,' how many would raise their hands?" The answer was "ZERO." And at that point, the #2 man said he "absolutely would NOT make a cold call." Frankly, the meeting deteriorated, the local boss and the visiting V.P. said little. Yours truly thanked them for time, wished them well and left the scene.

To my readers: I'm sure you can read between these lines. Consider these experiences and decide if and how anything shared with you might fit in your efforts to plan and conduct your personal/professional growth.

At this point, reflecting on the second actual situation, you might have said that the senior V.P. dropped the ball—failing to recognize a 'structural' impediment to the local profit center's growth prospects. Personally, as I reflect on what occurred, I candidly admit to failing to get some signals, jumping in and saying, "Hey, team, shouldn't we review some fundamentals?"

First, you do NOT want to run the risk of closing the operation, since you know this to be a growing territory. You know your company possesses valuable qualifications and service offerings for prospects your marketing people have identified. THERE'S ROOM IN THIS AREA FOR YOU! All that's left is deciding how to capture a reasonable, profitable market share!

Second, there are some business building basics that cannot be ignored or subordinated if this operation is to endure and grow. Push the pause button, stay cool and turn the meeting into a serious planning session! I expect you are NOT going to fold your tent and go away.

You are, indeed, here to stay and know that the geographic area that is your responsibility is enjoying positive growth. The public and private client prospects, according to your marketing folks, have needs for help that are consistent. So, it's time to consider and decide on how to refine your business plan, including staffing for growth, perhaps expanding your marketing department's responsibilities to include literal 'turning over the rocks' to identify specific client prospects and quantifying potential sales, consistent with your core competencies and professional services strengths.

You have to know the territory. Managing a team effort, led by marketing, to know the market for your services: what are the short and long-term growth prospects, leading a responsible effort to examine staff qualifications best prepared to capture new business.

And now, before we move to the next chapter, reflecting on 'Responsibility' and considering how many managers may be required, may we agree on some underlying team management fundamentals?

1. Break the big dream into defined goals, objectives, action plans, tasks.
2. Encourage team member input, leading to more informed and effective business strategies.
3. Respect each team member's role, encouraging the sharing of 'ownership.'
4. Focus on benefits, how shared ownership will beneficially advance the team's efforts.
5. Organize around developing a team spirit, focusing on cooperation.

CHAPTER FIVE

RESPONSIBILITY

For generations, in the military, authority could be delegated, but not responsibility. The commander of a squad, a platoon, a company, etc., could delegate authority to get something done, but NOT responsibility. Then came a change such that both authority and responsibility may be delegated, but not accountability. Ultimately, someone is always accountable for results.

Now think about our earlier discussion of the "upside down pyramid" of an organizational structure in which we put the accountable person, the boss, the principal in charge, the CEO, at the bottom to illustrate intent to bring out the best in each/every person above who occupies the layers of activity and responsibility. I stressed importance of that accountable 'boss' being able to delegate, assign and manage wisely, most competently. Giving each person every opportunity to excel, showing faith in potential while monitoring and being there to aid was the model I posed, again, to empower people to stretch, test themselves, and grow to exceptional professionals. And just to be totally clear, the 'boss,' though at the bottom of the pyramid in this model, is still accountable, meaning that that person has the final say and is indeed the person who will be relied upon for ultimate results of the team's or the company's successes or failures. Assuming all the members of the team, the branch office, and the division want to achieve the best results and believe those results reflect unanimous desire to 'bring out the best in people,' envisioning the upside-down pyramid can serve as a reminder of each individual's opportunity to contribute to winning!

Owners who lack knowledge, experience, and staff qualifications to recognize good and bad numbers when they see them would too often start down the road in trouble, finding themselves embroiled in disputes between architects and contractors, arbitration, litigation, over-budget messes, forced by deadlines, FF&E purchases they have made, hard limits of interim financing, all leading—too often—to cutting project scope, lobbing number of classrooms off the school program or "x" square footage (to the displeasure of the owner's employees) less vital to the organization's operation.

Yours truly earned gray hair from years of such experience, first as a subcontractor, then as a general, and finally, as a Program Manager/Owner Representative, encouraging and successfully. Changes in statutes that govern contract awards in the Public Sector are such that now the Owner can legally decide which General Contractor to whom a contract may be awarded based on qualifications: experience, financial strength, references, character, etc. Further, with changes in procurement statutes, came Owner awareness that the General Contractor can contribute his knowledge of systems, materials, methods, and costs during design to help the designers, avoiding errors and omissions, risks of cost overruns, budget 'busts,' and delays. Plus, such team operating efficiencies can yield greater profit for the architect, more harmonious, long term, productive relationships.

We're not what we think we are, but what we think, we are. Let's discuss the following scenarios:

1) In local government, should a non-engineer Public Works Director supervise the City Engineer?
2) In private consulting, should a non-engineer Project Manager supervise the Project Engineer?

Might this be the place to open a discussion of the various methods of contracting? After all, 'the buck stops' where accountability for bottom line results resides. In both the public and private sectors, elected officials, architects, engineers, developers, professional program managers, etc., someONE—even in a team context—is ultimately accountable for final results. Identifying that person, that firm, that company has consumed zillions of dollars in dispute resolution, arbitration and litigation over generations. Change order disputes, errors and omissions, fraud have prompted/encouraged thought about how approaches to project delivery can be modified from the traditional, age-old design bid build method of contracting to achieve satisfaction of Owner goals.

An unnamed general contracting firm made a practice of examining a set of plans and prints, once the decision was made to bid the job, dedicating serious time to identifying errors and emissions, estimating costs of same and then applying a percentage of those costs to their bid, so as to help assure the firm's being the low bidder, planning to lay change orders on the owner 'before the ink was even dry on their contract!' Inside that firm, a team of an architect and an estimator were responsible for reviewing the plans, documenting the errors and omissions, then pricing them. So, thinking it may be useful for you to consider the variety of contracting methods, you'll give it a shot, recognizing, again, that a perfect world doesn't exist, just as so many pros in the industry have admitted that no set of contract documents is perfect. All we can do is OUR BEST!

Your author contends there are four basic methods of contracting. Yes, there are variations of those, and you are encouraged to consider if and how a given delivery method may fit you on a given job, perhaps with some adaptation. Suggested is your drawing an illustration of each delivery method, showing lines of authority and contract responsibility.

Then, perhaps at the bottom of each illustration, cite the pros, cons and cautions. This can be used as a marketing tool, as a visual aid in presentations and interviews, and as an internal training aid or classroom teaching tool.

1. <u>Owner/Builder</u>: The Owner engages an architect and performs all the functions of a general contractor, contracting directly with all the subtrades. Risks include control of budget, schedule, documentation, changes in scope, errors and omissions, staffing, insurance, and bonding.

   Legality of this method is especially important in the public sector; statutes may prohibit adoption of this method beyond a given dollar amount of the cost of construction.

2. <u>Traditional Lump Sum Bid</u>: So familiar to all of us is this age-old contracting method, still commonly used, especially when the project is simple, perhaps smaller and the Owner's staff is well qualified to participate during design with timely, professional input so as to reduce change order risks and delays.

3. <u>Design/Build</u>: Stemming from the petro-chemical and petroleum industries wherein production is measured in barrels delivered, this contracting method evolved from interest in speed of project delivery, refining and simplifying reporting processes, and establishing a single point of contract responsibility.

4. <u>Construction Manager At Risk (CMAR)</u>: This method dates back to days of 'negotiated contracting' and owner-driven efforts to reduce risks of budget busts, schedule interruptions, disputes, litigation via selecting architects who positively embrace teaming with qualified general contractors to deliver benefits to clients of expedited design time, elimination of costly change orders, and early guarantee of total project costs through a guaranteed maximum price (GMP).

Chapter Six

Management

Who best runs the company? An organizational expert hired from beyond or an invested and loyal practitioner grown up from within the company's grass roots?

Suggested, really hoping you have read that opening statement regarding organizational expert or a loyal practitioner, etc., that you are saying something such as: "Wait a minute! You have confined this discussion to two, overly narrow and simplistic options! Obviously, the answer as to who best runs the company deserves discussion, consideration of THE leader profile that represents the best shot, LONG TERM, at building a successful company!" AND YOU'RE CORRECT...so let's dive in!

Leadership and qualities that YOU want demonstrated by the person at the helm include character, knowledge, passion, vision. 'Where can we go and what is a reasonable path to get there?'

Early in this book, it was acknowledged that "the construction industry ranks dead last in communication skills." Consider for a minute why that is true and what must be done to change that, for you, your firm, your company, and your team.

First, why dead last? Answer: perhaps related more to contractors than architects and engineers, a high percentage of construction companies in the country evolved from mom-and-pop operations. Grandfather founded the company, working 24/7 with his hands, learning a trade, working with the tools, literally, to build something. He passed that experience and knowledge to his children who grew the business by physically doing more and for more clients, continuing the pattern of reacting to clients' needs, thus limiting time for planning areas of personal and professional development. Business practices in areas of planning, marketing, human relations, and accounting were subordinated to physical work, thereby restricting internal/external focus on growth.

So, is it fair to condemn companies that are operating pretty much as they always have, not growing beyond a reactive approach to the markets they serve? Perhaps not. However, I am saying:

1. There will always be opportunities to grow via 'working with the tools' to create, solve problems, and make a living.
2. If the founders of a company or the management team of a company realize that some basic, perhaps organizational, structural changes are needed, how can that occur? Who leads? What must be the attitude with which the key individual or management nucleus considers change?

Here is a specific, real-world example of a company's founders' concluding that change in operating practices must occur in order to even maintain their penetration in the market they have served for several generations. The company is in the foods industry, producing edibles for retail distribution and public consumption. Over some years, the company observed its market share diminishing. Customers were moving to 'brand XYZ,' not due to lower pricing, but more efficient means of getting food to point of sale, plus some good old sales tactics of making sure the customers knew how much they are valued! So, the founders met with a management consultant who, ironically, came to the table with a construction management background.

At this point, frankly, you know 'the rest of the story,' as Paul Harvey used to say. Plus, I will add that the management team inside the foods company had to face reality: "If you continue to do what you've always done, the same way you've always done what you've always done, chances are you'll continue to get what you've always got!"

So, whatever your business, 'change' is not a four-letter word. If the market you intend to serve is dynamic (and I can't think of one that is not, at least to some even small, measurable degree), a manager's obligation is to be cognizant, vigilant and receptive. And YOU are a MANAGER, no matter what your position is on the totem pole!

And returning to strictly focus on the construction industry, valuing brevity and the time you give me for sincerely sharing some counsel, please consider the following:

- <u>Client Relations</u>: Maintaining loyalty—you to your client and the client's consistent reliance on you—involves communicating construction cost trends, economic development and industry highlights that may pertain to the specific client's business; personal notes, not being a pest or overdoing this, but showing interest in relationships beyond the project-specific issues.

- <u>"Value-Added" Performance</u>: Beyond the listing of services to be performed in a contract, are there ADDITIONAL short and long-term SERVICES you can provide, i.e.

programming, operations and maintenance, the client's capital program plans, etc.?

- <u>Professional Training and Education</u>: Exposing your staff to new, or better, more efficient means for use of tools, i.e. CAD, cost estimating software, proving company interest in helping employees to grow professionally, demonstrating added value to the clients, plus realization of greater profits.

- <u>Changing 'Barriers to Benefits'</u>: So often, firms, companies and teams are characterized or viewed as layered, compartmentalized, structured. If you see this or might see your firm trending in such a direction, consider ways efficiently to encourage internal cross-communication, i.e. the 'Marketing Department' and 'Operations.' Individual job satisfaction and personal/professional performance behaviors reflect on each and all job classifications within a firm. The employee who is not just empowered but encouraged—with planned inter-discipline meetings and exchanges—will feel valued and inclined to reflect that value to both family and clients.

- <u>As a 'Project Manager' or 'Principal in Charge'</u>: Trusting that you are in sync with your firm's short and long-term goals. In your private time—both individual employees and principals—are you comfortable assessing, planning your future? Are you 'equally yoked' with your counterparts, in position to meet, perhaps exceed, performance expectations?

- <u>'Engaged' or Treading Water</u>: By now you know that your author has the strongest desire for you to be successful, suggesting that attitude about your work, relationships and your future can be enormously important.

In *The Only Leadership Book You'll Ever Need*, Jane Flaherty and Peter Barron Stark explore what it takes to build workplaces where employees genuinely want to be. They emphasize that attitude and morale are not soft concepts. They directly influence customer satisfaction, productivity, and overall business performance. Firms and companies with higher morale outperformed others in the same industries by 11.3 percent!

I trust that you will know if an 'attitude adjustment' is in order. I pray that you are WINNING each and every working hour by being 'engaged.'

Chapter Seven

Follow the Money

Peel all the artichoke leaves away; at its heart, what 'makes the world turn'? What is the motivational influence most dominant in our behavior as individuals, as a political body, as a nation? Answer: wealth creation, capital, money! Someone else has it and you want it…or at least, and I will stress, you respect the most honorable, legal means according to which you can earn a share of wealth in achieving your individual and corporate goals.

Earlier considered was 'Lender Services' as an adjunct to your primary business as an architect, a contractor, etc., earning fees from interim lenders, banks and insurance companies, reviewing loan packages, conducting monthly inspections of construction progress, signing off on the contractor's monthly draw requests, etc. So, what does this service program have to do with 'following the money'? You want money, where do you go? Answer: (how about) 'to a bank!' Providing a service to a bank or other interim lender, i.e. insurance company, can expose you to borrowers such as developers who may become your client prospects.

Caution: should go without saying that you should expect NOT to serve both the lender and the borrower on the same project.

Trust me, having relationships with interim and long-term lenders can be so important to a firm's long-term growth. Consider this: banks, for example, will often have 'bad guy' lists internally; records of experience with borrowers they stay away from, and you should too! Sharing your business plan with your bank can expose you to new business prospects—the good guys!

And, now moving away from interim and long-term lenders per se, please consider how a city or a School District, for example, manages finances for capital programs approved by the public. An important Business Development strategy for you can be your getting to know the "FA's," the companies that serve in fiduciary capacities as Financial Advisors. Think about it: these companies compete for work in preparing bond issues, selling the bonds, managing the money. They know of, perhaps long before you, specific projects which need your services.

So, while obvious to you by now, what is the Business Development strategy: getting to know the FA's! Several of the most prominent are: RBC (Royal Bank of Canada), Piper Jaffrey and Stifel.

Lastly, considering for you some 'follow the money' strategies, we all have heard of Venture Capital sources: companies, individuals from 'angel investors' to investor partnerships, venture capitalists who are attracted to opportunities to fund start-ups, provide funding all the way from seed money to long-term capital commitments.

Two thoughts for you:

1. A prominent university hosts 'incubator' meetings to which start-up companies come to present themselves to V.C.'s; the exposure leads a hypothetical start-up to the beginnings of a relationship in which funding is negotiated, etc., etc.

2. And with further regard for you regarding V.C.'s, talk to your bank about the possibility of your bank's naming the Venture Capital folks they know and work with; people for you to know! Commonly, at minimum, an officer of a bank will have the responsibility to know the V.C.'s; at maximum, so to speak, a bank may assign client management responsibility to a department or V.C. officer so as to get the Venture Capitalist's business.

Now, a major shift from provision of your services to lenders, venture capitalists, etc., in following the money. Let's consider how capital projects in the public sector are funded and how you can benefit from that intelligence. Yes, I did refer to bond issues—you getting to know the financial advisors who prepare and sell the bond issues. There are strategies, however, you can use to 'be at the table' early, even earlier than the people who prepare the bond issues! So, what are some actions you can incorporate into your business plan?

No doubt you know, or are comfortable with educated assumptions, about directions of growth: cities, towns, counties, in the area of your offices or in the geographic areas of growth you are planning for your firm. Just listening to others in Chamber of Commerce meetings or reading the newspapers or talking with principals of firms with which you do business, i.e. subcontractors, sub-disciplines to your architectural practice, etc., you can make educated assumptions about targets of economic development. And, given that intelligence, rank the areas, contact the persons responsible for growth, introduce your firm, 'pick the brains,' prioritize for follow-up, and 'press the flesh.' Specific, representative job titles and persons who can help you know where growth can be expected to occur are: members of Boards of Supervisors, individuals whose job titles include Economic Development, City Manager and Council Member, and Public Works.

Who are the top five developers in the areas of growth you are planning for your firm? Getting the names and all other information you need for follow-up isn't difficult, then calling to identify yourself and your desire to know the leaders, investing both your time and the developer's time to share goals, your qualifications and your desire that a relationship be a 'two way street', not just a selfish opportunity to sound off about how great you are.

I would do you a disservice if, perhaps in this context of following the money, and in practical applications of my advice to you, I did not caution you to prequalify prospects carefully, avoiding the risk of wasting your time versus investing it. So many people come to mind; well-meaning individuals who have had dreams about developing properties or launching a business, people you might respect, good folks whose ambitions are laudable, whose ideas seem to make sense, but they haven't the money or experience to convert dreams to income streams.

I could tell you of one that stands out: a retired Air Force officer who recruited a handful of friends to join him in defining a two million square foot project, forming a partnership, preparing a pro forma, a schedule, an impressive 'package' as such material is called in real estate development circles, over some three years! What they did not consider is that they had NO experience in the field of real estate development. So, along came an individual who indeed had such experience, not as a developer but an engineer who had 'been there and done that' with schemers and dreamers over years.

Frankly, getting the attention of the key individual was a bit difficult. So much time and money had been spent in defining the project, talking to investors, friends and family, etc. Finally, it was necessary to state very directly that "you guys are not developers" and that's what is, and has been, missing!

Question to my readers: do I need to elaborate, spend time defining "developer" for you? Perhaps not, except to say that that individual, yes, is a visionary, is knowledgeable regarding steps that are taken in successful real estate development AND has access to the risk capital, private and institutional investors. Ideally, such a person or company has a portfolio of projects that are comparable in size. He's 'been there, done that' such that he can help prequalify the project, testing the logic before risking wasting time and more soft costs.

And one more thought about this for you: it's possible that the conceiver of the project, the one who has given birth to the dream, will be inclined to want to hold onto control as a developer is approached to join the team. It may be necessary to insist that the initial players prepare to take a back seat, even a minority interest, passing the real estate development baton to the experienced developer as a PARTNER vs. investor!

Chapter Eight

Final Thoughts

As a professional in the construction industry, you have one opportunity to make a good first impression, and that truth extends far beyond the jobsite. Maximize that moment each time it arrives. Your first impression becomes a lasting impression, shaping relationships, establishing trust, and setting the tone for long-term partnerships and positive results.

In a previous chapter, I emphasized the importance of communication. The words we choose convey a message to the client, participants in the project and fellow team members. Therefore, it is vital to incorporate words that encourage and inspire. Consider declaring the following statements daily:

- True leadership is not just about results. It is about who I become in the process.

- I lead, teach and motivate others with integrity, honor and probity, showing up as a caring, considerate and cooperative force within my organization.
- I apply what I've learned, continue learning, and never stop developing into the leader I am called to be.
- It is my mission to have good relationships, set goals, be organized, apply myself, maintain a positive attitude, follow through, and achieve the desired results.
- I display rectitude and am passionate about my endeavor.
- Every day presents an opportunity to apply my wisdom, to reflect on what is right and wrong, and to remain motivated.
- Through training, stamina and unwavering devotion, I will persevere, remain resilient and ultimately win—not just in title, but in character.
- I am consistent, ambitious and realistic, yet filled with hope.
- When I feel challenged, I do not lose sight of my goals. Instead, I ponder, adjust my reasoning and continue achieving.
- Success requires devotion to my vision, grounded in faith and belief, and guided by a clear plan.

- I remain organized in my planning, intentional in my tracking, and focused on progress.
- I build strong, relational connections by listening, acknowledging and valuing others.
- I am a true champion who leads with heart, is anchored in discipline, fueled by dedication, and refined through hard work, effort and persistence.
- My desire to serve has earned my client's trust. I will see their dream come to fruition.
- My team is rooted in service, love and respect to build something that lasts.
- I have the courage to stand firm when demand arises and determination to stay the course.
- I remain positive, gracious and determined.
- I AM A WINNER!

Organizing Your Presentation

Your presentation matters. Organize it as follows:

- HO HUM: That's the attention getter, that opening shot over the bough.
- WBTU: 'Why bring that up?'
- FOR INSTANCE: The substance, the 'meat' of the communication.
- SO WHAT?: This is the closing, obviously, the take-away, the point you want to make.

Reminders

1. The most selfish one letter word – "I."
   Avoid it.
2. The most satisfying two letter word – "We."
   Use it.
3. The most poisonous three letter word –
   "Ego." Overcome or kill it.
4. The best used four letter word – "Love."
   Value it.
5. The most pleasing five letter word –
   "Smile." Keep it.
6. The fastest spreading six letter word –
   "Rumors." Ignore them.
7. The hardest working seven letter word –
   "Success." Achieve it.
8. The most enviable eight letter word –
   "Jealousy." Distance it.
9. The most powerful nine letter word –
   "Knowledge." Acquire it.
10. The most valued ten letter word –
    "Friendship." Maintain it.

Notable Quotes

"Continuous effort, not strength or intelligence, is the key to unlocking our potential." ~ *Sir Winston Churchill*

"Failure always made me try harder next time." ~ *Michael Jordan*

"Adhere to your purpose and you will soon feel as well as you ever did...if you falter, and give up, you will lose the power of keeping any resolution, and will regret it all your life." ~ *Abraham Lincoln*

"The people you serve include the people you employ, as well as your customers. No matter how big your company grows, never forget what made you grow—listening to them...and satisfying them." ~*Harvey Mackay*

"A company that listens to its employees and clients can turn their whispers into winning strategies." ~ *Harvey Mackay*

"Leadership is not only having a vision, but the courage and discipline to get you there." ~ *George Washington*

"People who believe they can win will eventually win!" ~ *Roger Ailes*

Conclusion

In this book, I discussed developing a plan, having the right attitude, valuing relationships, how to gain new business, networking, the importance of marketing, how to see things from the owner's perspective, managing a project well, accountability, and the value in understanding all aspects of project finance. It has been my desire to have a positive impact on others in the construction industry by sharing the lessons learned over the years through experience and valuable relationships along the way. Hopefully, you have gained new insights into how to grow personally and professionally.

While writing this book, I have been constantly inspired, by the good Lord, to serve you in your pursuit of WINNING!

ABOUT THE AUTHOR

Richard A. Reese was born in Dayton, Ohio in 1934. His family moved to California in 1948. Mr. Reese's higher education is a business degree at San Jose State University and electrical engineering at State University New York.

His work experience began with General Electric in Indiana. He was later called to active duty at Ft. Benjamin Harrison in Indianapolis as an officer in U. S. Army (R.O.T.C.) Adjutant General branch. He was later deployed to South Korea before returning to civilian life. After getting settled back in the U.S., he found employment with Owens Corning Fiberglas in construction subcontracting. This led to being a principal of a large General Contractor, formation of a Program Management Division, and forming a Program Management (Owner Rep.) company. Mr. Reese has also published a paper in the Southwest Contractor titled *Finally Comes Project Management.*

Now retired, what prompted Mr. Reese to write a book titled *WINNING?* Over the years,

Mr. Reese has realized that CHANGE and MANAGING IT is fundamentally a characteristic of the construction industry. It is his desire to encourage all the participants involved in the process of project delivery to start and complete a project on time, to be on budget, to bring teams together and have everyone get along in order to meet the owner's goals.

It is your author's greatest hope that this book will serve all public and private sector readers toward those ends.